The
THREE
MOST POWERFUL
WORDS

DISCOVERING THE
FREEDOM OF RELEASING
THE ONES WHO HURT US

THE
THREE
MOST POWERFUL
WORDS

DISCOVERING THE
FREEDOM OF RELEASING
THE ONES WHO HURT US

DEREK PRINCE

ISBN 978-1-78263-424-9
Kindle 978-1-78263-367-9
ePub 978-1-78263-368-6
Product Code: T56EN3

Unless otherwise specified, all Scriptures are taken from
The Holy Bible, New International Version © 1978 by
New York International Bible Society.

All Scriptures marked NASB are taken from the *New
American Standard Bible* © The Lockman Foundation
1960, 1962, 1963, 1971, 1973.

All Scriptures marked KJV are taken from the *King James
Version* of the Bible.

This book is an edited transcript from *Derek Prince
Legacy Radio*, No. 056 "Forgiveness" by Derek Prince.

Derek Prince Ministries
www.derekprince.com

Contents

1

THE BLESSEDNESS
OF FORGIVENESS

Forgiveness is one of the most beautiful words in any language.

What makes this such a special and beautiful word? Well, consider some of the consequences that flow from forgiveness: reconciliation, peace, harmony, understanding, fellowship. How badly our world today stands in need of these things!

In contrast, consider some of the consequences that flow from our failure to forgive and to be forgiven: bitterness, strife, disharmony, hatred, and war. At times it seems as though the entire human race is in danger of being overwhelmed by these evil, negative forces. If we are ever to rise above these conditions, it will only be as we learn and apply the principles of forgiveness.

There are two directions of forgiveness represented in the Bible. These two directions are well portrayed by that great symbol of our Christian faith, the cross. The cross has two beams – one vertical and one horizontal. These two beams represent the two directions of forgiveness.

The vertical beam represents the forgiveness that we all need to receive from God and that can only be received through our identification with the sacrifice and resurrection of Jesus Christ. The horizontal beam represents our relationships with our fellow men, and it speaks of the forgiveness that in this case is two way: the forgiveness we need to receive from others and the forgiveness we need to give to others. Once again, the only place where we can receive the grace for that kind of forgiveness is *the cross*.

The Vertical

Let's begin with the type of forgiveness that we need and can receive from God Himself – the vertical aspect. There is such a blessedness in being forgiven by God. This is articulated perhaps most beautifully in Psalm 32, in which David says:

Blessed is he whose transgressions are forgiven, whose sins are covered. Blessed is the man whose sin the Lord does not count against him and in whose spirit is no deceit.

Psalm 32:1–2

In Hebrew this psalm begins with a plural word: *blessednesses.* "Oh, the blessednesses of the one whose transgressions are forgiven, whose sins are covered." The implication is that there are innumerable blessings attached to having our sins forgiven by God.

It is important to see that the Bible does not talk about a man who does not need forgiveness. The Bible clearly indicates that all of us need forgiveness from God. There are no exceptions. In another psalm, the psalmist says there is no man that does not sin. We have all sinned. Therefore we all need forgiveness. It is not a question of whether we *need* forgiveness but whether we *receive* forgiveness.

So David says, "Blessed is the man whose sin the Lord does not count against him and in whose spirit there is no deceit." He is writing about the type of man who has indeed sinned, but whose sin is no longer counted against him. Still, one absolute condition for receiving forgiveness is being absolutely honest with God. This means not trying to cover anything up, excuse anything, or hold anything back.

Then David writes out of his own personal experience:

When I kept silent, my bones wasted away through my groaning all day long. For day and night your hand was heavy upon me; my strength was sapped as in the heat of summer. Then I acknowledged my sin to you, and did not cover up my iniquity. I said, "I will confess my transgressions to the Lord" – and you forgave the guilt of my sin.

verses 3–5

I believe when David wrote this he had in mind the matter of Bathsheba, the wife of Uriah the Hittite. It was a terrible situation in which he committed adultery and then committed murder to cover up his adultery.

David obviously had been like many of us. For a long while he had refused to face the fact of his sin. He tried to ignore it. He tried to pretend that it never happened. He tried to cover it up. But all that time he was like a man with a burning fever. He said, "My strength was sapped as in the heat of summer. My bones wasted away."

The indication here is that there can be physical byproducts of holding on to unforgiven sin. A psychiatrist told me about a lady in one of the hospitals he attended who was in a hopeless condition. Her kidneys had ceased to function, her skin had turned pale yellow-orange, and she was in a coma, simply waiting to die.

As this psychiatrist walked past her bed one day, he was prompted by the Holy Spirit to speak – not to her conscious mind but to her unconscious. Her conscious mind was not able to receive anything from him. He said, "In the name of the Lord Jesus Christ, I remit your sins." And he wondered afterwards if he had done something foolish or whether the Holy Spirit had really prompted him.

To his amazement, about a week later he met the lady walking down the street in the city, perfectly healed! One cause of her physical condition was her unforgiven sins. When her sin was forgiven through this man's intercession on her behalf – when her spirit was clear with God – the way was open for her to be healed.

So, David's picture of his condition in Psalm 32 is very real. In the next verses David gives a personal application to this:

Therefore let everyone who is godly pray to you while you may be found; surely when the mighty waters rise, they will not reach him. You are my hiding place; you will protect me from trouble and surround me with songs of deliverance.

verses 6–7

David says, "Don't delay! While you have time, remember to turn to God and ask for His forgiveness. Then, when the trouble comes, when the waters rise, when calamities sweep over your life, you'll have a hiding place. You'll be kept safe in the hiding place of God."

The prophet Isaiah also has something urgent to tell us about our need to seek forgiveness from God:

Seek the LORD while he may be found; call on him while he is near. Let the wicked forsake his way and the evil man his thoughts.

Isaiah 55:6–7

There is only a certain period when you

can count on turning to the Lord. After that, it may be that the Holy Spirit will not prompt you again. It may be that you will never be moved again. But there is a moment when God may be found. There is a moment when God is near. Isaiah says, "Call on Him while He is near."

This is an urgent matter. If you have unforgiven sin in your life, *now* is the time to turn to God. The New Testament says, "Now is the accepted time" (2 Corinthians 6:2). Now is the time when God will hear you.

Don't delay, don't brush aside the gentle prompting of the Holy Spirit. Don't fight off that conviction that He brings upon you. Yield to His prompting. Call on the Lord while He is near. And remember the blessednesses of the man whose sins are forgiven.

Everyone Needs Forgiveness

Why do we need to be forgiven? Romans 3:23 very simply tells us why we must all seek forgiveness from God:

For all have sinned and fall short of the glory of God.

The word *all* would indicate that there are no exceptions there. All of us have sinned. There is not one righteous. There is not one who always does good.

You may argue and say, "Well, I've never committed murder or stolen or committed adultery or even gotten drunk." Maybe you can even say, "I've never told a lie." Maybe so, but there is one thing we all have in common. We have all sinned and, thereby, fall short of the glory of God.

The essence of sin is not doing some particular wrong thing. The essence of sin is robbing God of the glory that is due to Him from our lives. We have all led lives that robbed God of His glory. We have all led lives that were far below the level that God requires. We have fallen short of the glory of God. And there are no exceptions in this matter. All have sinned and fall short of the glory of God.

Wherever you may be, remember that the Scripture says to seek the Lord while He may be found. Call on Him while He is near. Don't let this day pass until you have sought God for forgiveness.

2

THE BASIS OF FORGIVENESS

This issue of forgiveness is of such vital, personal importance for each one of us, and the basis for forgiveness is the cross of Jesus Christ.

We can be forgiven only on the basis of what Jesus did on our behalf. More than seven centuries before Jesus suffered and died on the cross, the prophet Isaiah gave us a prophetic preview of what He was to do and why He was to do it. Although Jesus is not mentioned by name, all the writers and evangelists of the New Testament alike concur that Jesus is the one spoken of here – the nameless suffering servant of the Lord. In Isaiah 53 Isaiah describes the suffering death of our Lord Jesus Christ:

Surely he took up our infirmities and carried our sorrows, yet we considered him stricken by God, smitten by him, and afflicted. But he was pierced for

*our transgressions, he was crushed for our
iniquities; the punishment that brought us
peace was upon him, and by his wounds
we are healed. We all, like sheep, have
gone astray, each of us has turned to his
own way; and the Lord has laid on him*
[Jesus] *the iniquity of us all.*

Isaiah 53:4–6

That is the basis of God's forgiveness. It is
forgiveness that does not compromise His
justice. God's justice was fully and finally
satisfied because Jesus took our iniquity, our
rebelliousness and all our guilt.

Isaiah emphasises – as Paul does in Romans
3:23 – that none are excluded from the need of
forgiveness. "We all, like sheep, have gone
astray, each of us has turned to his own way."
Again, it is not exactly some terrible crime we
may have committed. It does not say we have
all committed murder or eaten too much. It says
we have gone astray. We have turned to our
own way. We have been rebellious. We have
been self-pleasers. We have lived by our own
standards. We have robbed God of His glory.
All of that is summed up in the one strong word
of Scripture: *iniquity*. But, thank God, the Lord
laid on Jesus the iniquity of us all.

The Hebrew word that is translated "laid on him" is very vivid. It means "made to meet together on him." All the sins, all the guilt, and all the burdens of all men, of all ages, of all races, past, present and future, came and met together upon the person of the Lord Jesus Christ as He hung on the cross. He did not die for His own sins. "He was pierced for *our* transgressions," Isaiah says. "He was crushed for *our* iniquities." "The punishment that brought *us* peace was upon *Him*."

Pay special attention to how close healing and forgiveness are. Many times people who are seeking healing really need forgiveness before they can be healed. Isaiah says, "The punishment that brought us peace." We see again that the consequence of forgiveness is peace, because Jesus was punished for our sin because He took our place. God offers us peace and reconciliation.

Can You Earn It?

In Romans 4 Paul bases his teaching on the experience of Abraham, the great forefather of the Jewish people of Israel. He points out that Abraham did not earn his relationship with

God. He was justified because he believed, not because of what he did.

What then shall we say that Abraham, our forefather, discovered in this matter? If, in fact, Abraham was justified by works, he had something to boast about – but not before God. What does the Scripture say? "Abraham believed God, and it was credited to him as righteousness." Now when a man works, his wages are not credited to him as a gift, but as an obligation. However, to the man who does not work but trusts God who justifies the wicked, his faith is credited as righteousness.

verses 1–5

If we lead perfectly good lives then we would have received the reward of righteousness as a due. But Paul says because none of us has led perfectly good lives, we cannot claim it as a due. We have to receive it out of God's graciousness as a gift.

Paul goes on to quote the words of David from Psalm 32. David says the same thing when he speaks of the blessedness of the man to whom God credits righteousness apart from works. That means we cannot earn it. There is nothing we can do to get it. "Blessed are they whose transgressions are forgiven, whose sins are covered. Blessed is the man whose sins the Lord will never count against him." Blessed words, "Never will our sins be counted against us."

Paul continues:

Yet he did not waver through unbelief regarding the promise of God, but was strengthened in his faith and gave glory to God, being fully persuaded that God had power to do what he had promised. This is why "it was credited to him as righteousness." The words, "it was credited to him" were written not for him alone, but also for us, to whom God will credit righteousness – for us who believe in him who raised Jesus our Lord from the dead. He was delivered over to death for our sins and was raised to life for our justification.

verses 20–25

The essence of receiving this forgiveness is having unwavering faith that God will do what He has promised to do. We have to believe those two aspects of the cross – that Jesus died as the penalty for our sins and was raised again to bring us justification.

Justified is one of those technical, theological words that calls for a little explanation. We are justified through faith and the death of Jesus on our behalf. I have always described *justified* as being "just-as-if-I'd" never sinned. Because when all my sins are forgiven, I am reckoned righteous with the righteousness of Jesus Himself.

Complete Forgiveness

One of the most wondrous aspects of God's nature is that when He forgives, He does not partially forgive. He totally forgives. Micah states this beautifully:

Who is a God like you, who pardons sin and forgives the transgression of the remnant of his inheritance? You do not stay angry forever but delight to show mercy. You will again have compassion on us; you will tread our sins underfoot and hurl all our iniquities into the depths of the sea.

Micah 7:18–19

Isn't that beautiful? Everything that we have ever done wrong – everything that could ever make us feel guilty, every accusation that the enemy could ever bring against us – God treads them underfoot and then hurls them into the depths of the sea.

Someone remarked once that when God casts your sins into the sea, He puts up a notice that says, "No Fishing!" Don't ever try to go back and resurrect something that God has buried. If God has forgiven you, you are forgiven. There are no questions. God's forgiveness is total. In Isaiah God speaks to His people:

"I, even I, am he who blots out your transgressions, for my own sake, and remembers your sins no more."

Isaiah 43:25

When God forgives us, He blots out the record. It is clean. It is just as though the thing that has been forgiven had never taken place. Not only does He blot out the record, but He blots it out from His own memory. He says that He will remember our sins no more.

God does not have a bad memory, but He does have the ability to forget. And when He forgives, He forgets!

3

RECONCILIATION IN TWO DIRECTIONS

Now that we have explored the wonder and totality of God's forgiveness, let's discover the other dimension of forgiveness – the horizontal direction of forgiveness. But before we can get anywhere in this chapter, you must accept one inescapable fact: it goes both ways. We need to forgive *and* we need to be forgiven by our fellow men.

This is very clearly set forth in the writings of Paul in Ephesians 2. He talks about the division in the human race, which was actually made by God Himself: the division between Israel (God's covenant people) and the Gentiles (the other nations). In the early Church, the Gentiles had come to be known by the Jewish people as "the uncircumcision," and they referred to themselves as "the circumcision." Paul says:

Therefore remember, that formerly you, the Gentiles in the flesh, who are called

"Uncircumcision" by the so-called "Circumcision," which is performed in the flesh by human hands – remember that you were at that time separate from Christ, excluded from the commonwealth of Israel, and strangers to the covenants of promise, having no hope and without God in the world. But now in Christ Jesus you who formerly were far off [the Gentiles] *have been brought near by the blood of Christ.*

Ephesians 2:11–13, NASB

What a terrible condition to be in – having no hope and without God. If you are without God, you certainly have no hope in this world – or in the next. But God did not let the matter rest there. Through Jesus Christ He offered forgiveness and reconciliation and hope. Not only to God's people, Israel, but to the entire Gentile world.

The shed blood of Jesus on the cross made a way for the Gentiles to find their way back to God from the depths of their ignorance, their shame and their licentious, horrible way of life. It is possible through the blood of Jesus Christ to come back to God.

Then Paul goes on to explain how this has changed all the relationships:

*For He Himself is our peace, who made
both groups into one, and broke down the
barrier of the dividing wall, by abolishing
in His flesh the enmity, which is the Law
of commandments contained in ordinances,
that in Himself He might make the two
into one new man, thus, establishing
peace, and might reconcile them both in
one body to God through the cross, by it
having put to death the enmity.*

verses 14–16, NASB

Notice that at the cross all barriers between humanity are broken down. There are no more divisions.

Paul uses the word *enmity* here twice. The first time, he speaks of enmity on the horizontal plane, between Jew and Gentile – enmity that in a certain sense was brought about by the Law that separated Israel and made them a distinct people from all other peoples. The second time he uses the word *enmity*, it is on the vertical plane. He is speaking about the enmity of the human race and its sin and rebellion towards God. He is saying that by Christ's death on the cross – at the very point where those two beams met – there was reconciliation in both directions. There was reconciliation from God to man and from man to his fellow man – both enmities destroyed by the cross. Paul continues:

> *He came and preached peace to you who were far away, and peace to those who were near; for through Him we both have our access in one Spirit to the Father.*

verses 17–18, NASB

The great message of the cross is forgiveness – and through forgiveness, peace. Isaiah 53 tells us the punishment that brought our peace was laid upon Jesus. When sin has been dealt with, forgiveness has been given. Then there is peace.

It is important to remember – especially in this strife-torn, bitter, hate-filled world – that the cross makes peace both from man to God and from man to his fellow man. All the barriers that kept man from having access to God are broken down. We who were far off have been brought near to God by the blood of Jesus.

The cross also eliminates the barriers between man and his fellow man. The separations, the divisions, the enmities, the suspicions, and the mistrusts all have been dealt with by that one single act of God – the death of Jesus on the cross. I believe that in this world of ours today no message is more desperately needed than the message of what was accomplished on behalf of the entire human race by the death of Jesus on the cross. He has made us all the children of God, irrespective of race or religious background or any other difference. When we receive Jesus, we all have access by the one Holy Spirit to God as our Father.

In Colossians Paul gives us another picture of the outworking of this reconciliation achieved by the cross:

> *Do not lie to each other, since you have taken off your old self with its practices and have put on the new self, which is being renewed in knowledge in the image of its Creator. Here there is no Greek or Jew, circumcised or uncircumcised, barbarian, Scythian, slave or free, but Christ is all, and is in all.*

Colossians 3:9–11

The old self died in Jesus on the cross. The Scripture says our old self, our old man, was crucified with Him (Romans 6:6). That was dealt with. That old rebel was put to death there on the cross. Paul now says that since you have taken off your old self and its practices, and have put on the new self, which is being

27

renewed in knowledge in the image of its Creator, that the image of God that was marred by man's sin is being restored.

He goes on to say that every kind of barrier, separation and division in the human race – the barrier between the Jew and the Gentile, between the religious and the non-religious, between the educated and the uneducated, between the employer and the employee, between classes, between races – all have been abolished.

It is interesting what Paul says in light of this. It is a timely message for today's Church. He begins by saying, "Do not lie to each other." We have to put off any kind of deceit, mistrust or dishonesty. If we want to be the people He created us to be, we need to be absolutely open with one another as God's people.

I often think of Noah's ark. God made provision for the preservation of a selected number of every kind of animal from the old order before the world was plunged beneath the flood. God supernaturally caused them to come to Noah – and at a certain point they went into the ark. Many of those animals were by nature at enmity with one another. They preyed upon one another – they killed one another and they feared one another. But inside the ark there was peace. Have you ever thought about that?

The ark is an Old Testament picture of being in Christ. No matter what background you have – or what kind of attitudes you had – when you come into the ark, they are done away with. You are a new creation. You have a new relationship.

There is peace where there was once strife and disharmony. All have been replaced by the peace of God through the reconciliation of Jesus on the cross.

4

THE UNFORGIVING SERVANT

Let's look more closely at the necessity of our forgiving one another. The importance of this truth to the successful Christian life cannot be overstated. Jesus Himself lays special emphasis on the necessity to forgive others. In Matthew 6:9–15 He says:

This is how you should pray: "Our Father in heaven, hallowed be your name, your kingdom come, your will be done on earth as it is in heaven. Give us today our daily bread. Forgive us our debts, as we also have forgiven our debtors. And lead us not into temptation, but deliver us from the evil one." For if you forgive men when they sin against you, your heavenly Father will also forgive you. But if you do not forgive men their sins, your Father will not forgive your sins.

Of all the sections of The Lord's Prayer, it is interesting that the only passage about which

Jesus thought it worthwhile to make specific comment was the one on forgiveness. Notice that He lays down the proportion in which we can ask forgiveness from God. It is in the same proportion in which we forgive others. "Forgive us our debts, as we also have forgiven our debtors." If we totally forgive others, we can ask God totally to forgive us. But if we withhold total forgiveness to others, then we cannot claim total forgiveness from God.

Then Jesus interjects, "For if you forgive men when they sin against you, your heavenly Father will also forgive you. But if you do not forgive men their sins, your Father will not forgive your sins." No language could be clearer than that. Do we want God to forgive us? Then we have no option; we must forgive others. There is no alternative.

In Mark 11 Jesus is speaking about how to get our prayers answered:

Therefore I tell you, whatever you ask for in prayer, believe that you have received it, and it will be yours. And when you stand praying, if you hold anything against anyone, forgive him, so that your Father in heaven may forgive you your sins.

Mark 11:24–25

When we pray, Jesus puts on us the responsibility to forgive others. He does not say, "Wait until they come and ask for your forgiveness." He says, "If you want your prayers to get through to God, you take the initiative. Forgive those other persons."

In most cases, I do not believe it is even necessary to go to them and tell them. But you have to release them, because as long as you hold them in their debts to you, God is holding onto your debt to Him. And your debt to God is infinitely greater than the debt any human being owes you.

Jesus says, "Forgive him, no matter what he has done." His language is so complete. "If you hold anything against anyone, forgive him." Anything against anyone. That leaves out nothing and no one, doesn't it?

There is no situation or circumstance in which we can justify refusing to forgive others. Jesus is saying that when you pray, believe that you receive what you are praying for as you pray. But, He says, there is a potential problem: when you stand praying, if you hold anything against anyone, forgive him so that your Father in heaven may forgive you your sins.

Do you have unanswered prayers? Have you felt sometimes that you were crying out and

God's ears were stopped against your prayer? Perhaps God has been waiting for you to learn the lesson that if you want Him to hear your prayers you must begin by forgiving anybody that you may be holding anything against.

Jesus goes deeper into this in His parable of the unforgiving servant. It is so vivid – and it has such important lessons for all of us:

Then Peter came to Jesus and asked, "Lord, how many times shall I forgive my brother when he sins against me? Up to seven times?"

Jesus answered, "I tell you, not seven times, but seventy-seven times.

Therefore, the kingdom of heaven is like a king who wanted to settle accounts with his servants. As he began the settlement, a man who owed him ten thousand talents was brought to him. Since he was not able to pay, the master ordered that he and his wife and his children and all that he had be sold to repay the debt.

The servant fell on his knees before him. 'Be patient with me,' he begged, 'and I will pay back everything.' The servant's master took pity on him, canceled the debt and let him go.

But when that servant went out, he found one of his fellow servants who owed him a hundred denarii. He grabbed him and began to choke him. 'Pay back what you owe me!' he demanded.

His fellow servant fell to his knees and begged him, 'Be patient with me, and I will pay you back.'

But he refused. Instead, he went off and had the man thrown into prison until he could pay the debt. When the other servants saw what had happened, they were greatly distressed and went and told their master everything that had happened.

Then the master called the servant in. 'You wicked servant,' he said, 'I canceled all that debt of yours because you begged me to. Shouldn't you have had mercy on your fellow servant just as I had on you?' In anger his master turned him over to the jailers until he should pay back all he owed.

This is how my heavenly Father will treat each of you unless you forgive your brother from your heart."

Matthew 18:21–35

I worked out once what those debts were, using the rate of the dollar to silver that was current at the time (and of course that fluctuates). The first debt was about six million dollars. A servant who owed six million dollars was brought to the king. In contrast, using the same ratio, the fellow servant's debt to the first servant was worth about seventeen dollars. So we are talking about seventeen dollars versus six million. The first servant's unforgiveness, not his debt, earned him a prison sentence. At the most basic level, unforgiveness is a prison.

Notice that Jesus did not leave the moral of this parable up to the listener. He applied it specifically to each of us. He said, "If you don't forgive your fellow believers, your fellow human beings, as you want God to forgive you, God will deal with you like the master dealt with that unforgiving servant."

What a sober warning! It comes straight from the lips of Jesus. No one was more ready to forgive and be gracious than Jesus, but He set a very clear principle in place here. If you want to be forgiven by God, you must forgive others.

Three Keys

Three important points emerge from this parable. First of all, unforgiveness is wickedness. The master said to the servant, "You wicked servant." That's a harsh indictment, isn't it? The servant had not committed a heinous crime; he had simply failed to forgive his fellow servant. It appears that in God's opinion, failure to forgive is wickedness.

Second, Jesus says that the master was angry. Unforgiveness provokes God's anger. Remember, there is an exact parallel between the master and the servant and with God and each of us.

My third observation is that unforgiveness imprisons us. One translation calls the jailers "tormentors" (KJV). Jesus said, "My heavenly Father will deal with you exactly as that master dealt with his servant." That unforgiving servant was delivered to the tormentors.

There are multitudes of God's people in the hand of tormentors today because they fail to forgive somebody. Some have mental torment, some have spiritual torment, some have physical torment. There are many different kinds of torment. But one sure result of unforgiveness is torment. Let me urge you to make it your aim to forgive as you want God to forgive you. Many people say, "I can't forgive." But that is not true. You can, if you know how.

5

HOW TO
FORGIVE OTHERS

In The Lord's Prayer, Jesus said, "Forgive us our debts, as we forgive our debtors." He tied us down to not expecting forgiveness from God in a greater proportion than we forgive others.

When confronted with this requirement to forgive others as we want God to forgive us, I have often heard people say, "I can't forgive." But this arises from a misunderstanding of the nature of forgiveness. Forgiveness is not an emotion; it is a decision. You cannot work up the *emotion*, but you can make the *decision*. This means that you can forgive if you know how. I believe there are six simple steps you can take to successfully walk out genuine forgiveness.

Recognise

The best first step is to recognise your need to forgive. Be honest with yourself. Stop being so religious. Do not pretend that there are no bad feelings anywhere in your heart. Acknowledge that there are some people you really are bitter against, that you really hold resentment against them. Recognise it. Don't cover it up. Be willing to name the person.

I have learned that unforgiveness and resentment are usually directed towards the people closest to us. You do not often find yourself resenting the woman who delivers your mail. She does not get close enough. But the people who share the same house with you? The person who shares the same bed with you? That is where we are so prone to resentment, bitterness, and unforgiveness. Be willing to acknowledge to yourself the person or persons whom you need to forgive.

Submit

Second, do not resist God. You have to submit to both His Word and His Spirit. Wrestle through and accept what His Word teaches. God asks, "Do you want Me to forgive you? Forgive that other person. I'll forgive you in the same proportion that you forgive the other person."

Remember, in God's economy, the other person only owes you seventeen dollars, but you owe God six million. Do the math. Decide for yourself whether it is really worthwhile to forgive that seventeen-dollar debt. On its lowest level, forgiving others is not a matter of being tremendously spiritual – it is really a matter of self-interest. Any person who would not forgive seventeen dollars for the sake of being forgiven a debt of six million is just not good at arithmetic! I am not asking you to be a spiritual giant. I am just telling you how to take care of your own best interest in this matter of forgiving others.

You also need to submit to God's Spirit. The Holy Spirit brings conviction. The uneasiness or discontent you feel when you think about certain relationships is often the Holy Spirit prompting you to forgive. Do not ignore that prompting. Listen to the Holy Spirit.

Decide

Once you have submitted to God's Word and His Spirit, the next thing you need to do is make the right decision. Remember, do not wait for feelings. Your feelings are not fully under your control. But your will *is* under your control. Forgiveness proceeds from the will, not from the emotions. Choose to forgive that person or those persons. Make the decision. "I forgive. I will forgive. I do forgive."

Declare

The next step is one of the most important. Affirm your forgiveness verbally. Do not just let it be an inner thought that passes through your mind. Say it out loud with your mouth. "Lord, I forgive. I forgive my spouse. I forgive my mother-in-law. I forgive my children. I forgive my grandchildren. I forgive the pastor. I forgive the neighbour."

Whoever it is, say out loud that you forgive them. And if it does not sound right the first time, say it again. Maybe say it louder. Maybe say it over and over. Saying it with your mouth gives it tremendous power.

Stand Strong

Assuming that you have been willing to make the first four steps – to recognise your need, submit to God, make the right decision, and affirm it verbally – the next two steps are safeguards against the return of resentment.

Suppose you start thinking again about that particular thing that was so hard and so bitter in your life. Are you supposed to forgive again? My advice would be to not do that – because I believe it weakens your first forgiveness.

When you are tempted to go back to resentment or bitterness, remind yourself and God that you have already laid the issue to rest. Say, "Lord, I have already forgiven that person." Put it in the past. You have forgiven. It is finished. Whatever that person's seventeen dollars represents – consideration, satisfaction, love, respect – it *has been forgiven*. The IOUs have been torn up. You cannot get them back. They are scattered to the wind.

Pray and Bless

The final step in this process of forgiveness is to replace the negative with the positive. Whenever you begin to think of that person that you had such a problem forgiving, do not dwell on their bad points. Do not go back to all the bad things they have said and done. Thank God for them. Thank God you have forgiven them. Think of anything that is good about them, and begin to thank God for that. Then pray for them.

Pray for God's best for them. Pray for God to pour out His favour on them.

Let's review the steps to walking out forgiveness:

1. *Recognise* your need to forgive.

2. *Submit* to God – to His Word and what it teaches; to His Spirit as it pleads with you.

3. Make the right *decision*.

4. *Declare* out loud and, if necessary, find a witness – somebody who will actually hear you make that statement.

5. *Stand strong* in what you have done. Do not go back to resentment.

6. *Pray and bless* to replace the negative with the positive. Think well of that person. Pray for them. Ask God to bless them. Every time you do something positive, you make less room for the negative.

I want to finish by giving you a model prayer that you can pray when you need to forgive somebody else. Read it carefully. Make it your prayer. Use it whenever you need to forgive:

Lord, I acknowledge my need of Your forgiveness. I believe You are willing to forgive me for Christ's sake. But I also acknowledge that I need to forgive others. And so, by a decision of my will, I forgive _____ [specifically name the person or people you need to forgive]. *I now forgive him/her as I would have You forgive me.*

Trusting in Your grace and faithfulness, I now affirm that I have forgiven and You have forgiven me. Thank You, Lord. I pray this in the name of Jesus. Amen.

While these six steps themselves may be simple, putting them into practice may not be easy. As you learn to walk them out, I believe you will experience increasing freedom and blessing from the Lord.

ABOUT THE AUTHOR

Derek Prince (1915–2003) was born in India of British parents. Educated as a scholar of Greek and Latin at Eton College and Cambridge University, England, he held a Fellowship in Ancient and Modern Philosophy at King's College. He also studied several modern languages, including Hebrew and Aramaic, at Cambridge University and the Hebrew University in Jerusalem.

While serving with the British army in World War II, he began to study the Bible and experienced a life-changing encounter with Jesus Christ. Out of this encounter he formed two conclusions: first, that Jesus Christ is alive; second, that the Bible is a true, relevant, up-to-date book. These conclusions altered the whole course of his life, which he then devoted to studying and teaching the Bible.

Derek's main gift of explaining the Bible and its teaching in a clear and simple way has helped build a foundation of faith in millions of lives. His non-denominational, non-sectarian approach "Keys to Successful Living" has made his teaching equally relevant and helpful to people from all racial and religious backgrounds.

He is the author of over 50 books, 600 audio and 100 video teachings, many of which have been translated and published in more than 100 languages. His daily radio broadcast is translated into Arabic, Chinese (Amoy, Cantonese, Mandarin, Shanghainese, Swatow), Croatian, German, Malagasy, Mongolian, Russian, Samoan, Spanish and Tongan. The radio programme continues to touch lives around the world.

Derek Prince Ministries continues to reach out to believers in over 140 countries with Derek's teachings, fulfilling the mandate to keep on "until Jesus returns." This is effected through the outreaches of more than 30 Derek Prince Offices around the world, including primary work in Australia, Canada, China, France, Germany, the Netherlands, New Zealand, Norway, Russia, South Africa, Switzerland, the United Kingdom and the United States. For current information about these and other worldwide locations, visit www.derekprince.com

BOOKS BY DEREK PRINCE

Philosophy, the Bible and
the Supernatural
Power in the Name
Power of the Sacrifice, The
Prayers and Proclamations
Praying for the Government
Promise of Provision, The
Prophetic Guide to the
End Times
Protection from Deception
Pulling Down Strongholds
Receiving God's Best
Rediscovering God's Church
Resurrection of the Body*
Rules of Engagement
Secrets of a Prayer Warrior
Self-Study Bible Course
(revised and expanded)
Set Apart for God
Shaping History Through
Prayer and Fasting
Spiritual Warfare
Surviving the Last Days
Thanksgiving, Praise
and Worship
They Shall Expel Demons
Three Most Powerful
Words, The
Through Repentance to Faith*
Through the Psalms with
Derek Prince
Transmitting God's Power*
Three Messages for Israel
Two Harvests, The
War in Heaven
Where Wisdom Begins
Who is the Holy Spirit?
Will You Intercede?
You Matter to God
You Shall Receive Power

Get the Complete Laying the Foundations Series*

1. Founded on the Rock (B100)
2. Authority and Power of God's Word (B101)
3. Through Repentance to Faith (B102)
4. Faith and Works (B103)
5. The Doctrine of Baptisms (B104)
6. Immersion in The Spirit (B105)
7. Transmitting God's Power (B106)
8. At the End of Time (B107)
9. Resurrection of the Body (B108)
10. Final Judgment (B109)

Derek Prince Ministries
www.derekprince.com

DEREK PRINCE MINISTRIES OFFICES WORLDWIDE

DPM – Asia/Pacific
38 Hawdon Street, Sydenham
Christchurch 8023,
New Zealand
T: + 64 3 366 4443
E: admin@dpm.co.nz
W: www.dpm.co.nz and
www.derekprince.in

DPM – Australia
Unit 21/317-321
Woodpark Road, Smithfield
New South Wales 2165,
Australia
T: + 612 9604 0670
E: enquiries@derekprince.com.au
W: www.derekprince.com.au

DPM – Canada
P. O. Box 8354 Halifax,
Nova Scotia B3K 5M1,
Canada
T: + 1 902 443 9577
E: enquiries.dpm@eastlink.ca
W: www.derekprince.org

DPM – France
B.P. 31, Route d'Oupia,
34210 Olonzac,
France
T: + 33 468 913872
E: info@derekprince.fr
W: www.derekprince.fr

DPM – Germany
Söldenhofstr. 10,
83308 Trostberg,
Germany
T: + 49-8621-64146
E: IBL.de@t-online.de
W: www.ibl-dpm.net

DPM – Netherlands
Nobelstraat 7-08
7131 PZ
Lichtenvoorde
Phone: (+31) 251-255044
E: info@dpmnederland.nl
W: www.derekprince.nl

DPM – Norway
P. O. Box 129
Lodderfjord
N-5881, Bergen,
Norway
T: +47 928 39855
E: sverre@derekprince.no
W: www.derekprince.no

**Derek Prince Publications
Pte. Ltd.**
P. O. Box 2046,
Robinson Road Post Office,
Singapore 904046
T: + 65 6392 1812
E: dpmchina@singnet.com.sg
English web: www.dpmchina.org
Chinese web: www.ygmweb.org

DPM – South Africa
P. O. Box 33367
Glenstantia 0010 Pretoria,
South Africa
T: +27 12 348 9537
E: enquiries@derekprince.co.za
W: www.derekprince.co.za

DPM – UK
PO Box 393,
Hitchin, SG5 9EU
UK
T: + 44 (0) 1462 492100
E: enquiries@dpmuk.org
W: www.dpmuk.org

DPM – Switzerland
Alpenblick 8
CH-8934 Knonau,
Switzerland
T: + 41(0) 44 768 25 06
E: dpm-ch@ibl-dpm.net
W: www.ibl-dpm.net

DPM – USA
P. O. Box 19501
Charlotte NC 28219,
USA
T: + 1 704 357 3556
E: ContactUs@derekprince.org
W: www.derekprince.org

Other books by Derek Prince

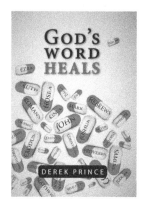

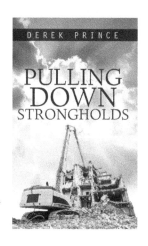

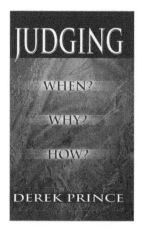

Lightning Source UK Ltd.
Milton Keynes UK
UKHW020833061219
354840UK00013B/815/P